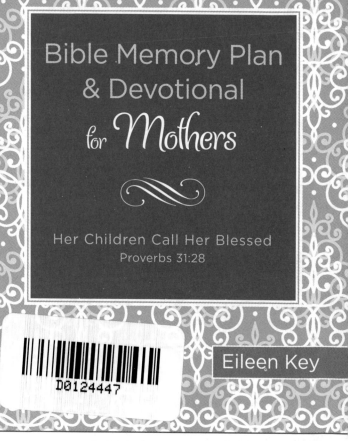

Bible Memory Plan
& Devotional
for Mothers

Her Children Call Her Blessed
Proverbs 31:28

Eileen Key

BARBOUR BOOKS
An Imprint of Barbour Publishing, Inc.

Published by Barbour Books, an imprint of Barbour Publishing, Inc., P.O. Box 719, Uhrichsville, Ohio 44683, www.barbourbooks.com

Our mission is to publish and distribute inspirational products offering exceptional value and biblical encouragement to the masses.

Member of the
Evangelical Christian
Publishers Association

Printed in the United States of America.

Especially for

....

From

....

Date

....

FOR
Sarah, Rachel, and Dawn

Contents

*D*o you ever feel as if there are not enough hours in the day to accomplish all you need to do? As a mom you wear so many hats, it's hard to keep them on the hat rack! Shopper, cook, maid, chauffeur—and the list goes on. Where is the "me" time?

And throw into the mixture memorizing scripture? Oh my. Too big a task!

But what can soothe your heart, cool your frustrations, and give you a closer relationship to the heavenly Father better than remembering His love letter given to you? At times we require encouragement and guidance. If you've stored His Word in your mind, you have the words printed indelibly on your heart and can pull them forth to use in any situation. The *Bible Memory Plan and Devotional for Mothers* is intended to give you confidence and pass on ideas for recalling what God has spoken. Each encouraging devotion is followed by a page with scripture verses to memorize and some ideas that will help you make memorization a happy habit.

Don't feel a spirit of condemnation or take this idea as an assignment—see it for what it is: a guidebook to help you hear what the Lord has spoken. Penned on the pages of the Bible is the map to a more contented life.

So turn the page, and let's begin this journey that is different every day.

Child of the King

And as far as sunrise is from sunset,
he has separated us from our sins.
As parents feel for their children,
GOD feels for those who fear him.
He knows us inside and out.
PSALM 103:12–13 MSG

*O*ur children are extensions of the love God has poured into us. When we realize what He sacrificed when He gave up His Son for our sins and try to imagine giving up one of our own, it's an impossible concept to grasp. But grasp it we must.

To lead our children in His way, we must first be assured we are on His path. By praying and asking Jesus into our hearts, we begin an incredible walk as children of the King. Once our salvation is secure, we may enable our children to see our walk of faith. We can't save them, but we can give them a good role model to follow.

From Page to Heart

. . . .

The only mistake you can make with scripture memorization is to quit. To kick-start remembering these first two important, life-changing verses, write them on several colored index cards. Place these cards in visible places: the bathroom mirror, the window over the sink—places your eyes will catch the color and cause you to take note of the words. Say them aloud. When you read and hear the Word, it sticks in your brain more easily. Don't quit! Don't stumble and fall. But if you do, try and try again. Begin with these fundamental words that tell how much God loves you.

*For God so loved the world that he
gave his one and only Son,
that whoever believes in him shall not
perish but have eternal life.*
JOHN 3:16 NIV

Accepting the reality of this verse marks
the beginning of new life in Christ—your life and
possibly the lives of your children. Read the words
to them and explain what the Lord has done to
save you. Even little ones can sense the excitement
in a mother's voice. Make this a memorable time
for them; you are their role model.

*Wash away all my iniquity
and cleanse me from my sin.*
PSALM 51:2 NIV

Knowing the limitless love of the Savior,
and that He will be with you when difficult
times come, can get you through life's
obstacles. You are a child of the King,
and He is always ready to listen and help.
Begin today. Allow the Holy Spirit to
be your teacher as you learn the Word.

Loving Our Loved Ones

But from everlasting to everlasting
the Lord's love is with those who
fear him, and his righteousness
with their children's children.
PSALM 103:17 NIV

To wear the title *mom* indicates you are in charge of a child or children. What a daunting task. Even those at your breakfast table can be unlovely and difficult. But knowing God has given you the responsibility of caring for a person (or people) should allow you to breathe easier, for He will equip you to handle the job as you lean on Him.

His love is infinite. His love can allow you to feel affection for even the unlovely. Through Him you may choose to forgive, forget, and love.

Love is a word we bandy about and use in so many forms. But God's love—the love of the Father—is immeasurable

From Page to Heart

. . . .

*A*re you ready to remember more of His love letter, to learn of His continuing love, which scripture records? Did you know. . .

Love is patient, love is kind. It does not envy,
it does not boast, it is not proud.
1 CORINTHIANS 13:4 NIV

Most moms say "I love you" often to their children. God does the same. He's your *Abba,* "Father," and He loves you. His written Word repeats that over and over. He is patient and kind, even when we fail.

Squabbling kiddos? You can be the same way. Friends, spouses, or children might be unlovable at times. Yet you can learn the following lesson:

"Love one another. As I have loved you,
so you must love one another."
JOHN 13:34 NIV

You love your children, even when it is not easy. Memorizing these words will enable you to bring thoughts of pure love to the forefront of your mind when your tasks aren't easy.

If it is possible, get an accountability partner. Read the verses to your partner and have that person repeat the verses to you. Practicing out loud helps our brains absorb the words more readily.

But the fruit of the Spirit is love.
GALATIANS 5:22 NIV

Learning the love letter enables you to become closer to the Lord. If you do not have someone to help you, try a digital recorder—most phones have one these days. Speaking and hearing scriptures at bedtime is relaxing and will help you remember more. Upon waking, repeat the process. At the breakfast table, dinner table, or any other gathering with your kiddos, repeat the words to them. Let them know you are learning God's Word so you may impart more love to them.

Sovereign Lord, you are God!
Your covenant is trustworthy.
2 SAMUEL 7:28 NIV

~≈~

*E*ach day we have the opportunity to put our trust in the Lord, to walk in the path He has set forth. It's often easier to trust in Him for ourselves; it's usually an altogether different feeling to trust for our children or others. Trusting in the heavenly Father to take care of them, to provide for them—isn't that giving up control?

Exactly.

God wants us to lean on Him, to follow His pathways. Sometimes that means walking practically blindfolded because we cannot see what is around the next turn. This is not an easy way to live, having blind trust. However, if we choose to do so, we will see His mighty plan at work in the long run.

Give Him your hand and let Him lead you on an exciting, wonderful journey.

From Page to Heart

* * * * * * * * * * * * * * * * * * * *

What mom can't use a helper? Christians have the Holy Spirit living within them, and He is known as the Helper. Now is the time to ask for His assistance in remembering the Word of God. Pray for wisdom and clarity as you concentrate on the "trust scriptures."

Those who know your name trust in you, for you, Lord, have never forsaken those who seek you.
Psalm 9:10 NIV

Now focus on the word *trust*. Scripture tells of many who trusted in the Lord. Hannah trusted in the Lord for a child. David hid in the caves and relinquished control of his life to the Lord. Peter trusted Jesus to help him walk on water. Paint these pictures in your mind. Visualize many individuals with outstretched hands, then put yourself in the center of that painting. Realize you are going to trust in Him and carve His instructions on your heart.

Trust in the Lord forever, for the Lord, the Lord himself, is the Rock eternal.
Isaiah 26:4 NIV

Extend one hand and turn it palm up, your mind still on the word *trust*. Reach for Him. Tell Him you want to trust, and repeat the scriptures out loud several times. Once you feel He holds you, turn your hand over, surrendering to the heavenly Father for your care and the care of your children. Think of how you might apply these words this very day, and, in faith, trust the Holy Spirit to help.

Our Hope Is in the Lord

I wait for the LORD, my soul waits,
and in his word I hope.
PSALM 130:5 ESV

Synonyms for *hope* include*: look forward to, anticipate, and wish*. Moms experience these feelings often. We want good things for our children and families and can dream big dreams. God understands that. He puts a measure of optimism in our hearts when we rely on Him. This doesn't mean He is a magic genie who fulfills all wants and desires. No indeed. He knows what is best for each of us, for He created us.

Don't stand to one side and tap your foot, expecting a quick answer. His plan doesn't always unfold that way. Instead, live with expectation and great faith in a heavenly Father who wants the best for you.

With the guidance of the Holy Spirit, the possibilities for you and your children are worth waiting for.

From Page to Heart

• •

*H*aving hope seems to be a natural thing for mothers. We hope so much for our children: their health, their relationships, their futures. So learning the wonderful words of life concerning hope should come easy to us.

Now faith is confidence in what we hope for and assurance about what we do not see.

HEBREWS 11:1 NIV

Say these words out loud. Repeat them in the shower, in the car, wherever you can. Read it and love it. Set your mind on hope and allow the Holy Spirit to begin His work in your heart. On "blue" days, make it a priority to read these scriptures. Notice it says we have confidence and assurance. So be confident and assured. His Word tells you to be. Use these scriptures as starters for prayer time and personalize the verse. You have things for which you hope.

Lord, it tells me in Your Word to place my hope in You. I choose to do so this day. Please help me rely on You and wait with expectation and faith for_____.

Relax and let your mind wander over the prayer
and the scripture. Smile. Reach. Trust. And hope!
This isn't a timed test. It's a test for all time!
And hold on: unswervingly!

Let us hold unswervingly to the hope we profess,
for he who promised is faithful.
HEBREWS 10:23 NIV

Work in Progress

*We do not dare to classify
or compare ourselves with some
who commend themselves.*

2 CORINTHIANS 10:12 NIV

Look to the right, look to the left. Am I doing this right? What a tendency moms have to compare their styles of rearing children to the ways of other moms. Scripture states that is not something we should do.

No two children are alike. No two families are alike. The only way you should measure yourself is by godly standards. And you will often fall short there, but do not despair. Do not beat yourself up over any mistakes. Instead, pick yourself up and try again.

The Lord sees your heart. He knows when you are trying, and He is always willing to forgive. After all, He created you. He put your very desires and talents and skills inside of you and equipped you for the job of being a mom!

From Page to Heart

. . . .

Moms unite! Do you have an accountability partner? Someone with whom you might share these memory verses? Because we know women often have a "compare and contrast" attitude. Sharing these verses and discussing them, focusing on the idea that God's not finished with us, is an uplifting experience.

God, who began the good work within you,
will continue his work until it is finally finished
on the day when Christ Jesus returns.

PHILIPPIANS 1:6 NLT

If we choose to compare ourselves to others, we make a mighty mistake. We don't know the faults anyone else possesses. We can't make those kinds of judgments. We only see the outside. And how deceptive that might be.

Fixing our eyes on Jesus,
the pioneer and perfecter of faith.
HEBREWS 12:2 NIV

Instead of looking at "the Joneses," fix your eyes on the One who died for you. He found you perfect! And He understands it takes great courage and faith to face the "I-fall-short" image that invades your mind. Those feelings are just that: feelings. Not facts.

Start small, mustard-seed small.
And know the Holy Spirit will help you grow.

*"Truly I tell you, if you have faith as small as a
mustard seed, you can say to this mountain,
'Move from here to there,' and it will move.
Nothing will be impossible for you."*
MATTHEW 17:20 NIV

Go, Child, Go!

*May the God who gives endurance
and encouragement give you
the same attitude of mind toward
each other that Christ Jesus had.*
ROMANS 15:5 NIV

$\mathcal{I}$f you are a sports fan or have a child who participates in a sport, you are probably familiar with sideline cheerleading. Or maybe you currently play a sport where others cheer you on. There's nothing like hearing your name hollered from the sidelines by a fan to spur you on as you play.

Imagine your Abba, Father, above as He cheers you on in life. He wants the very best for you and sent His Word, inspired by the Holy Spirit, so you may read words of encouragement, of support. He wants you to know He's got your back!

From Page to Heart

. . . .

Our children need to feel we support them as they make decisions each day. Whether it's tiny "well-done" notes stuck in their lunch boxes or pats on the back after a ball game, a caring, loyal mom who offers encouragement will help propel them toward excellence. Children are a gift, and they need care and love. What better way to help them tap into their potential than offering up words of deserved praise?

Therefore encourage one another
and build each other up.

1 Thessalonians 5:11 NIV

Our youth are faced with many decisions in today's culture. Teaching them to turn their thoughts toward Jesus, toward the heavenly Father, lets them know they can face any storm and gives them a solid rock on which to stand. Let's offer them words of life!

A song penned in the 1800s says: "Sing them over again to me, wonderful words of life; Let me more of their beauty see, wonderful words of life. Words of life and beauty, teach me faith and duty."

Wonderful words of life will help keep your child on God's path.

But encourage one another daily,
as long as it is called "Today."

HEBREWS 3:13 NIV

Choose this day to drink of this scripture deeply, so it washes over you until you realize the great promises given in the Word for you and your family. Know of His faithfulness. Feel His presence. Encourage each family member with beautiful words of life.

To Tell the Truth

"Whoever belongs to God hears what God says."
JOHN 8:47 NIV

*W*hat channel do you watch or what newspaper do you read to search for the daily news? And are you sure what is printed or said is actually truth? In our society, it's often difficult to ascertain the correct facts in any given situation. So it's amazing to know words penned long, long ago in the Bible are the real, honest-to-goodness, you-can-bank-on-it truth.

God knew mankind would need a directory, an answer to life's difficulties. And He handed us a manual. However, often it's the last place we look for solutions. We can Google, go to YouTube, and select any number of explanations for questions, yet overlook the real truth written in His Word.

There's an app for that: reach for the Word when you have a question, and let the truth set you free.

From Page to Heart

· ·

Mothers want truth-telling kids. That's a fact. It takes a lot less energy to deal with any given problem when you just get to the bottom of it with the truth. No skirting around issues—just the facts, please. We want our children to be honest citizens, to be conscientious and trustworthy. Telling the truth is a step in that direction.

An honest answer is like a kiss on the lips.
PROVERBS 24:26 NIV

So it is with our heavenly Father. He already knows what you're up to, what you've said or done, but He wants to hear from you. Tell Him your worries and your concerns. Be honest. Are you angry at Him? Frustrated with life? Tell Him. He can handle the truth. Do your best to learn these words. Repeat them to your children so they know the importance of truth.

Guide me in your truth and teach me, for you are God my Savior, and my hope is in you all day long.
PSALM 25:5 NIV

And when your children are ready, lead them toward Jesus and let them see He is the truth! Show them these words:

"Then you will know the truth,
and the truth will set you free."
JOHN 8:32 NIV

Guide your children so they might know that
having Jesus change your life for eternity
is the ultimate freedom and truth.

Reaching Out

Each of you should use whatever gift you have received to serve others, as faithful stewards of God's grace in its various forms.
1 Peter 4:10 NIV

Turn on the television, flip the pages of a newspaper, and many examples of devastation and loss can be found. From hurricanes and earthquakes to house fires and the death of loved ones. No matter where we go, we cannot avoid the plight of others.

God, in His infinite mercy, has given each person a gift. We need to find ours and use it. Let's begin in our homes! Ask the Holy Spirit to reveal your gift. Search His Word to determine what He wants you to do.

Help another; for you never know when you might need another's help. Embody Jesus. Let your light shine forth for His glory.

From Page to Heart

. . . .

*"So in everything, do to others what you
would have them do to you."*

MATTHEW 7:12 NIV

The Golden Rule! Yes, it is in the Bible.
In Matthew we see Jesus sitting on the
mountaintop speaking to crowds and encouraging
them to live the Golden Rule. He knows their
limitations yet encourages them to reach out!

We need to teach His words to our children.
Focus on this scripture for a few days. Let your
children give examples of how they can follow
the idea behind it. Encourage them to be kind,
thoughtful, and giving, even to a sibling.

"In the same way, let your light shine before others, that they may see your good deeds and glorify your Father in heaven."

MATTHEW 5:16 NIV

❧

Bragging rights over being generous are not to show how awesome we are, but rather how great our God is. It is His Holy Spirit within us that we want people to see. Not us, but Him.

Drawing a lighthouse on the front sidewalk with chalk can be a fun way to discover and understand the true meaning of Christ's teaching. He wants us to become beacons to our neighbors, and He wants you to be a beacon to your family, a shining light that reaches out with His love in all directions.

Making Our Plans

But the plans of the LORD stand firm
forever, the purposes of his heart
through all generations.
PSALM 33:11 NIV

❧

*A*rmed with our ideas and plans, we moms
wake up and set out to continue our jobs:
to rear well-adjusted, wonderful, intelligent
children. Then we walk into the kitchen and see
messy faces, dirty dishes, and piles of laundry.
What happened to the plan for the family?

Often we set the bar so high—based on
comparisons sometimes—that we will never
achieve the greatness we have desired.
Instead of the desire to overachieve, be real.
And turn to the heavenly Father, who wants
to guide you in every step of your day.

Pray: *Dear Lord, lead me and guide me*
on this journey. Show me how You see my
family and myself. Forgive my shortcomings
and instruct me on the way to go. Thank You,
Lord. Amen.

From Page to Heart

. . . .

*W*hen we firmly root ourselves in the Word of God and know without a shadow of a doubt that He has plans for us, then we can trust Him to direct our every step. Lifting our eyes to Him, the Author and Finisher of our faith, we can pray and ask for specific direction.

"For I know the plans I have for you," declares the LORD, "plans to prosper you and not to harm you, plans to give you hope and a future. Then you will call on me and come and pray to me, and I will listen to you."

JEREMIAH 29:11–12 NIV

Write this scripture over and over until it is committed to memory. These words will carry you far in life, for they are a promise! Now that doesn't necessarily mean the "hope and future" is the one on your bucket list. This is when we must fully understand that God has a plan and no matter what it looks like, we will walk it out.

Teach these words to your children at an early age so they can rest in the Father's love. Show them by example how to call on Him in prayer. Kneel at their bedside and repeat the memory verse. Pray it over each member of the family.

*For through him we both have access
in one Spirit to the Father.*
EPHESIANS 2:18 ESV

Rescued in Time

He rescued me from my powerful enemy.
2 SAMUEL 22:18 NIV

We might not face a powerful, armed enemy like warriors of old. We might, however, face enemies from within. Fear, anger, addictions—whether drug or food—and other "demons" may cause us to struggle and fight. So fear not, for the Lord is with you (see Isaiah 41:10).

God put the Holy Spirit within us to help us in any struggle we might have. When we try to resist and fight back in our own strength, we will often fail. From that loss, we spiral down into depression. The fight is on again: circles and circles of unseen enemies sent to attack our beliefs and discourage us.

Stand firm! Know the heavenly Father stands beside you, invisible yet full of strength. He will help fight any battles we face. He is always by our side. What better armed force could there be?

From Page to Heart

. . . .

He brought me out into a spacious place;
he rescued me because he delighted in me.
PSALM 18:19 NIV

Look into the mirror and see yourself unafraid. Is that too much to ask? If so, repeat Psalm 18:19 over and over. Use a washable magic marker and write the words on the mirror so you may learn them. Know the Lord delights in you. *Delight*—a delicious word. It means "pleasure, happiness, gladness, satisfaction." The Creator delights in you, whom He has fashioned.

Don't let doubt cloud your understanding of His Word. Stand firm in your beliefs. Hide the words inside yourself, so that when you are swayed by feelings and emotions, you may pull strength from memory. It becomes an easier task to be unafraid.

"Here is my servant whom I have chosen, the one I love, in whom I delight; I will put my Spirit on him, and he will proclaim justice to the nations."
Matthew 12:18 niv

These words quoting the prophet Isaiah tell of
the coming King. But you may apply these words
to yourself. Announce to your children that the Lord
God put His Holy Spirit within you once you were
saved. Tell them of His wondrous deeds, and repeat
this verse often. Chosen—the Everlasting Father
has chosen you! Love—*Abba,* Father, loves you!
Rejoice! For He is with you.

Forgive One Another

"And forgive us our debts, as we also have forgiven our debtors."

MATTHEW 6:12 NIV

⌇⌇⌇

The words memorized in the oft-repeated Lord's Prayer should speak to our hearts and help us release anything we harbor against another. We need to let it go. Yet this task does not come easily to man.

Lewis B. Smedes wrote in his book, *Forgive and Forget*, "When you release the wrongdoer from the wrong, you cut a malignant tumor out of your inner life. You set a prisoner free, but you discover that the real prisoner was yourself."

Release your "enemy" and know you have followed God's will. It doesn't necessarily mean you have forgotten the problem, but you've made a choice motivated by the Holy Spirit to move on and share grace. Forgive by faith, whether you feel like it or not. Obey God's Word.

From Page to Heart

. . . .

Bear with each other and forgive one another
if any of you has a grievance against someone.
Forgive as the Lord forgave you.
COLOSSIANS 3:13 NIV

Tell your brother [or sister] you're sorry."
"Say 'I'm sorry.'"

These are commands we moms use to admonish
and encourage our children. And not one of those
commands comes naturally to a child. They're
commands that must be taught and reinforced—by
word and example. The last six words of Colossians
3:13 are ones we can repeat to our children when
we chide them for holding on to a grudge. The
Lord forgave you, so you must forgive one another.
Repeating the scripture and having them recite it will
engrave it into their minds. Then help your children
know what this verse means by praying together.

*Then Peter came to Jesus and asked, "Lord,
how many times shall I forgive my brother
or sister who sins against me? Up to seven
times?" Jesus answered, "I tell you, not seven
times, but seventy-seven times."*
MATTHEW 18:21–22 NIV

❧

This scripture teaches us that we are to forgive
an unlimited number of times. Certainly not what
our kiddos (or we) want to hear. Yet as we learn
to invite the Lord into our day and allow the Holy
Spirit to guide us, our hearts soften. Resentment,
which once overwhelmed, begins to subdue. Our
Abba, Father, holds us close and lets us abide in
His love.

Father, help us forgive as You have forgiven us. Thank You, Holy Spirit for helping us accomplish this goal. Amen.

Purposeful Thanks

"The LORD is my strength and my defense;
he has become my salvation. He is my God,
and I will praise him."
EXODUS 15:2 NIV

Circumstances can jerk our focus from our heavenly Father and cause us to grumble instead of praise. It's just natural for us to do so. Therefore, we need to purposefully rise in the morning, turn our faces heavenward, and say, "Thank You, Lord." Put on an attitude of gratitude to begin your day. Waking up is a gift!

A sense of praise creates a rainbow in our spirits. We can more readily recognize the goodness of the Lord and become aware of the Holy Spirit's presence. So raise your hearts and hands and shout out praise to your Abba, Father!

From Page to Heart

. . . .

I will sing the LORD's praise,
for he has been good to me.
PSALM 13:6 NIV

Shout for joy to the LORD, all the earth. Worship the
LORD with gladness; come before him with joyful
songs. Know that the LORD is God. It is he
who made us, and we are his; we are his
people, the sheep of his pasture.
PSALM 100:1-3 NIV

Ready to sing? In the book of Psalms, we are encouraged to lift our voices to the King of kings. Put a tune to the words above, which will help you memorize the scriptures. Our Father is our strength when we are weak and can't do one more thing. He hears our groans and feels our pain. Praise away!

Know in the depth of your being that once you give your heart to Jesus, you are one of His lambs. Nothing can snatch you from His arms; He is the shepherd who will care for you. That knowledge should cause your heart to swell with gratitude. A song of praise will surely be on your lips.

Praise be to the God and Father of our Lord Jesus Christ! In his great mercy he has given us new birth into a living hope through the resurrection of Jesus Christ from the dead.
1 PETER 1:3 NIV

New birth, new hope in Him.
Most assuredly He is worthy of our praise.

*Though he may stumble, he will not fall,
for the Lord upholds him with his hand.*
PSALM 37:24 NIV

❧

None of us have a perfect life. We "stumble" along and try to do right each day, but no matter what, we make mistakes. Whether they are errors of judgment, choices leading us to sin, or forgetfulness that trips us up, mistakes can cause pain to us and others.

How grateful we are to know our Abba, Father, is quick to forgive when we ask. Scripture states He upholds us with His hand, meaning He has a grip on us that won't let go. In Isaiah 43:5 (NKJV) it says: "Fear not, for I am with you." That mantle of fear that cloaks us can be shed when we realize the Lord is our guide. He offers His forgiveness as soon as we ask.

Ask your heavenly Father to forgive you today.

From Page to Heart

* * * * * * * * * * * * * * * * * * * *

For all have sinned and fall short
of the glory of God.
ROMANS 3:23 NIV

Therefore, there is now no condemnation for those
who are in Christ Jesus.
ROMANS 8:1 NIV

When our children goof, make an error or mistake, we certainly don't throw them out with the day's trash. We might have to grit our teeth and turn away for a few minutes to get over some anger, but we love our children despite what they may have done. So it is with our heavenly Father.

Hide these scriptures in your heart. Don't just memorize them, *know* them. Begin to understand the depth of God's forgiveness. All have sinned, even you, yet He loves you! He sent Jesus to die for you! Nothing you can do can snatch you from His hand. And He does not condemn you for past mistakes.

If we confess our sins, he is faithful
and just to forgive us our sins, and to cleanse
us from all unrighteousness.
1 JOHN 1:9 KJV

Show your children several different colored pencils.
Stress that despite the differences, the pencils
all have one thing in common: they have erasers.
Those erasers are used to remove mistakes.
When we ask for God's forgiveness, it's as though
a giant eraser comes and removes what we have
done. Just as an eraser cleanses a wrong answer
from a sheet of paper, our prayer asking
for God to forgive us will do the same.

Rest Within

Yes, my soul, find rest in God;
my hope comes from him.
PSALM 62:5 NIV

*D*id you trudge through this day, so weary it was hard to take a step? Often we find ourselves exhausted—and it's not always a physical exhaustion that can be remedied by a good night's sleep. Often it's a heart-heavy weariness.

When we are tied up in knots, unable to concentrate or sleep, we must make a choice and shift our focus to the Lord and His goodness. It's not easy on cloudy days. It takes inner strength and courage. Be encouraged by the Word. Thank our Creator, knowing full well He has a plan.

Do you think this exhaustion takes God by surprise? Of course not. He knows our hearts, and He knows how best to minister to us. Be of good cheer. The Lord is in control.

From Page to Heart

. . . .

*Whoever dwells in the shelter of the Most High
will rest in the shadow of the Almighty.
I will say of the LORD, "He is my refuge
and my fortress, my God, in whom I trust."*
PSALM 91:1–2 NIV

*He gives strength to the weary and increases
the power of the weak.*
ISAIAH 40:29 NIV

As moms, scriptures about weariness and rest resonate within. Our very job description means we are going to, at times, be beyond exhausted—so tired it's hard to open our eyes. Yet what better task could be before us than to care for our little ones? What a privilege it is to be a mother. We should receive a badge of courage.

Psalm 91 speaks of resting in His shadow. Find something outside that casts a long shadow and stand there. Feel the difference? In heat, a shadow offers comfort from the sun. Consider God's love just like that: a covering. His mighty hand hovers over you, not to strike you down but to shelter you, caress your face, and uphold you when you stumble.

Go to Him when the burdens are too much.
Repeat His words over and over until they are
part of you, until your heart can cry out, "Abba,
Father, thank You for Your everlasting love and care."

God's Promises

His divine power has given us everything we need for a godly life through our knowledge of him who called us by his own glory and goodness. Through these he has given us his very great and precious promises.

2 PETER 1:3–4 NIV

❧

*W*hen we give our word, our promise, we expect to carry out whatever we said we would do. However, it's easy to forget in time. We aren't very good at always keeping our promises.

What a marvelous thing to know: our God never goes back on His Word. All He has promised He will do. Don't be discouraged if you feel a promise hasn't come through. Realize God's timing isn't ours. He holds the sands of time and sifts them through His fingers. We have to wait, secure in the knowledge that our Abba has made a promise.

Easy? Not at all. Worth it? Definitely!

From Page to Heart

. . . .

The LORD is trustworthy in all he promises
and faithful in all he does.
PSALM 145:13 NIV

Not one of all the LORD's good promises
to Israel failed; every one was fulfilled.
JOSHUA 21:45 NIV

Mommy promises are often those we toss out to our kiddos just to get them to settle down. "Yes, you may have ice cream. Yes, I promise." Only to discover none in the freezer! Whoops! It's not always an intentional step of not following through. More often it's a half-thought-out idea—a hollow promise. Then we dance around and try to make excuses for falling short.

Our God doesn't act like that. This is where we take a stand, just like the old-time hymn "Standing on the Promises." We rest in Him, "listening. . .to the Spirit's call, resting in my Savior as my all in all."

Write down His Word and meditate on the meaning of His promises. He said He would ____ [and fill in the blank]. Scripture tells us He is trustworthy and will not fail. If God said He would do it, He will! Period.

Write out the word *fulfill*. Jot down synonyms: *complete, accomplish, execute, perform, implement, finish.*

Understand how clearly the Lord states His words
and come to know His heart, and you will see
His desire is to fulfill, accomplish, or finish what
He has said He would do! Be encouraged! The Lord
will see you through all your circumstances.
For. He. Has. Promised. Period!

Bitterness or Resentment

*Get rid of all bitterness, rage and anger,
brawling and slander, along with every form
of malice. Be kind and compassionate
to one another, forgiving each other,
just as in Christ God forgave you.*
EPHESIANS 4:31–32 NIV

*P*our a dot of food coloring into a glass
of water. The entire volume of liquid is
discolored. So it is when we foster bitterness
or resentment. It's one thing to say, "Forgive
and forget," yet it's quite another feat to
accomplish that task. However, unless we
want to be "discolored," it's something we
must strive to do.

Once you've recognized the bitter "root"
taking hold, it's time to deal with it. Start on
your knees, confessing to the Father this hold
on you. Take it to Him in prayer. Let the Holy
Spirit begin His work within your heart.

Ask Him to help you forgive and heal
from the hurt. He is ready and willing.

From Page to Heart

. . . .

"For if you forgive other people when they sin against you, your heavenly Father will also forgive you. But if you do not forgive others their sins, your Father will not forgive your sins."
MATTHEW 6:14–15 NIV

Bickering children, impatient spouses, clamoring relatives, neighbors who drive you to distraction: all can become sources of resentment and bitterness. When you feel these emotions well up inside, it's tempting to give in and grumble. You look for justification in your situation. Maybe you turn to a friend with your complaints, and she takes up your offense, adding fuel to the fire. Time to step back and assess the situation before it's completely out of hand. Once bitterness has the opportunity to grow in your heart, it's very easy to become unloving.

God wants the best for His children. Write these scriptures on note cards. Take a walk and recite them out loud. Shrug your shoulders and imagine anger and unforgiveness sliding away. These negative emotions can take a physical toll, so it's in your best interests to give them up.

[Love] does not dishonor others, it is not
self-seeking, it is not easily angered,
it keeps no record of wrongs.
1 Corinthians 13:5 NIV

Forgiveness is the key to bitterness extermination.
The forgetting part takes longer, for we humans
tend to hang on to the past. Instead, focus on the
future—on a clean break from the past hurt—and
praise Him. For praise can chase away the hurt.

Friendship

A friend loves at all times.
PROVERBS 17:17 NIV

❧

The well-known writer C. S. Lewis stated: "Friendship is unnecessary, like philosophy, like art. . . . It has no survival value; rather it is one of those things which give value to survival."

Friends need to be chosen carefully and loved. True and lasting friendship can happen in a moment, just as it did to Jonathan and David in 1 Samuel 18:1 (NLT): "After David had finished talking with Saul, he met Jonathan, the king's son. There was an immediate bond between them, for Jonathan loved David."

Proverbs 18:24 (NIV) tells us to seek to become a friend: "One who has unreliable friends soon comes to ruin, but there is a friend who sticks closer than a brother." True friendship is always worthwhile. Our life is enhanced when we have good friends who walk alongside us through good days and bad.

From Page to Heart

. . . .

For since our friendship with God was restored
by the death of his Son while we were
still his enemies, we will certainly
be saved through the life of his Son.

ROMANS 5:10 NLT

Who better to be our Friend than Jesus? He is reliable, trustworthy, and loving. He holds you in the palm of His hand. A true walk with Him enriches your life. The hymn "What a Friend We Have in Jesus" continues on with these words: "all our sins and griefs to bear! What a privilege to carry everything to God in prayer!" We can know He listens. He doesn't have to be online, on Facebook, or tweeted. He's right beside us all the time.

*"There is no greater love than to lay down
one's life for one's friends."*
JOHN 15:13 NLT

It is good to share life with another. And mom-to-mom time strengthens you. Discussing life's "battles" over a cup of tea releases emotional stress and begins to create a special bond of trust. For introverts, it's difficult to seek a friend, so ask the Lord to send someone.

*God is faithful, who has called you into fellowship
with his Son, Jesus Christ our Lord.*
1 CORINTHIANS 1:9 NIV

Use a friend to help you in your memory work.
Read the Bible with someone and learn His Word.
Let that person know how important planting the
Word deep within can be, for all of the pages point
to God's faithfulness and love.

*I will praise God's name with singing,
and I will honor him with thanksgiving.*
PSALM 69:30 NLT

〜

*W*ake in the morning with a heart of thanksgiving. Before you plant your feet on the floor, give voice to praise. For He alone is worthy. God has done so much for us. It started with your salvation and continues on as He cares for you. Have a heavy heart? Then find one thing for which you can say, "Thank You, Lord." Maybe it's the sunshine or much-needed rain. A promotion, retirement, or the sound of your child's laughter.

Everywhere in the world are thankful droplets raining upon us, if we just take the time to recognize them. Our Abba, Father, wants much for us, but most of all, He desires our praise and adoration, our thankful attitude.

Be of good cheer, He is near to you.

From Page to Heart

. . . .

Give thanks to the LORD, for he is good;
his love endures forever.
1 CHRONICLES 16:34 NIV

*H*um the words to the hymn "Count Your Blessings" (find the lyrics on YouTube) and feel your heart lift as you do just that: count your blessings, one by one! List your salvation, your children, your family, your home. Whatever circumstance you are in, the Lord is there beside you, and if you search, you can find a reason to thank Him.

Let the peace of Christ rule in your hearts,
since as members of one body you were
called to peace. And be thankful.
COLOSSIANS 3:15 NIV

Use the tune to sing the scriptures on thanksgiving. Pour the words into your heart and mind so when difficulties arise, they're available to call upon. As scripture says, "Shout for joy to the LORD" (Psalm 100:1 NIV). Maybe it's in the shower stall or in your car, but you can shout no matter where you are!

*Give thanks in all circumstances; for this
is God's will for you in Christ Jesus.*
1 THESSALONIANS 5:18 NIV

It's said that Mom is the heart of a home, so if your heart is full of joy, that joy will overflow to those around you. The most precious possessions you have—your kiddos— will experience the bubble of thanksgiving within you. Go ahead. Try it out. Let the Lord know how thankful you are. Sing to Him a new song!

LOL

*Yet I will rejoice in the LORD! I will be joyful
in the God of my salvation!*
HABAKKUK 3:18 NLT

To rejoice is to celebrate and be pleased about something. We can take delight in knowing the Lord our God cares about us. When we are aware of God's great goodness, then we can laugh and fill our hearts with joy.

Healthy laughter is a wonderful gift from God. He grants us the ability to laugh out loud at ourselves in the safety of family and friends. Some health centers have used laughter therapy to help patients begin to heal.

If you are suffering under a dark cloud, look for ways to laugh more. It might be just the prescription you need. And when you do laugh out loud, send up a silent "thank You" to our Father in heaven for this blessing: the gift of laughter.

From Page to Heart

. . . .

We were filled with laughter, and we sang for joy.
And the other nations said, "What amazing
*things the L*ORD *has done for them."*

PSALM 126:2 NLT

∞

People seem to be attracted to those who have
a cheerful countenance and happiness within.
God has created us so that we might have joy, and
if we embrace His Word, we can claim that joy.
Search out scriptures that speak of laughter and
joy, happiness and peace. They are there to be
learned and experienced.

O clap your hands, all ye people; shout unto God
with the voice of triumph.

PSALM 47:1 KJV

Children are blessed when their mom is filled with laughter and happiness. As the old saying goes, "If Mom is happy, then all are happy."

Chuck Swindoll stated, "Laughter is the most beautiful and beneficial therapy God ever granted humanity." If God created it, then surely it is good.

Rejoice in the Lord always.
I will say it again: Rejoice!
Philippians 4:4 NIV

Have you giggled today? Listen to a giggling child:
it's contagious! Repeat Philippians 4:4. Have you
sung? Make up a tune for Psalm 126:2. God inhabits
the praises of His people. Be determined to look for
reasons to share your joy and let the Word resound
from within! Clap your hands as you read Psalm 47:1.
Make a joyful noise unto your heavenly Father. He
surely will smile. And maybe you'll giggle.

Praise be to the God and Father of our Lord Jesus Christ, the Father of compassion and the God of all comfort, who comforts us in all our troubles, so that we can comfort those in any trouble with the comfort we ourselves receive from God.
2 CORINTHIANS 1:3–4 NIV

L ife cannot be experienced without some sorrow. But no matter the circumstances, you can trust that the Creator of the universe is in charge of your life and cares. He wants to walk with you through this valley. He sent the Holy Spirit to be your Comforter.

Draw near to Him. Hear His heartbeat and cry on His shoulder. He will dry your tears. In the psalms, David says, "I will lift up mine eyes unto the hills, from whence cometh my help" (Psalm 121:1 KJV). Have you lifted your eyes? Do so now.

From Page to Heart

· ·

*The Lord is close to the brokenhearted
and saves those who are crushed in spirit.*

PSALM 34:18 NIV

People need to grieve. If you are in the depths of a sorrowful experience, don't put a timetable on your grief. Allow yourself time to heal on your own terms. As you do so, words of encouragement can be found in scripture. Look for them, even when you feel you cannot lift your head.

*You will keep him in perfect peace, whose mind is
stayed on You, because he trusts in You.*

ISAIAH 26:3 NKJV

Copy one verse for the week and concentrate on it. Absorb the meaning behind the words, the context. Jesus will speak to your heart through the Holy Spirit to begin a healing process. Once those words sink in to the depth of your soul, write another and learn it. Let the Word be a balm applied to your sorrow.

"Let not your hearts be troubled.
Believe in God; believe also in me."
JOHN 14:1 ESV

Turn your eyes upon Jesus and know you have a
blessed hope in Him because you are His child.
He sees each hurt and ache. Just as moms do when
their children fall, He wants to soothe and console
your weary body and mind. Allow Him to ease your
burden and relieve you of pain. Jesus cares.

Attitude Opportunities

*For seven days they celebrated with joy
the Festival of Unleavened Bread, because
the LORD had filled them with joy by changing
the attitude of the king of Assyria so that
he assisted them in the work on
the house of God, the God of Israel.*
EZRA 6:22 NIV

*R*emember the storybook *The Little Engine
That Could*? What a great attitude: "*I think
I can, I think I can, I think I can.*" Adopting this
feeling will help us focus on the present. We
can "at this moment" do whatever God has
asked.

In Ezra, scripture tells of a king whose
attitude God changed. When we ask Him, He
can take a negative and turn it into a positive
every time. So when you're feeling off-kilter,
talk to the Father. He gets it. He'll listen and
help you "in the work on the house of God."

From Page to Heart

. . . .

*You were taught. . .to put off your old self. . . .
to be made new in the attitude of your minds;
and to put on the new self, created to be like
God in true righteousness and holiness.*
EPHESIANS 4:22–24 NIV

Thought police: This morning, did you awaken
with positive thoughts? Did you say, "Good
morning, Lord, thank You for another day"? Or was
a grumble on your lips? What was your outlook for
the day?

*For the word of God is alive and active. Sharper
than any double-edged sword, it penetrates even
to dividing soul and spirit, joints and marrow;
it judges the thoughts and attitudes of the heart.*
HEBREWS 4:12 NIV

Scripture encourages us to think on the good instead of dwelling on the negative. Not so easy, surely. However, when we recognize what contentment can do for us physically, it's certainly something for which we should strive. Proverbs tells us a cheerful heart is good medicine! And it often takes a "sword" to divide the ungrateful attitude from the grateful one.

Finally, brothers and sisters, whatever is true, whatever is noble, whatever is right, whatever is pure, whatever is lovely, whatever is admirable—if anything is excellent or praiseworthy—think about such things.
PHILIPPIANS 4:8 NIV

Focus today on slipping into that new skin!
Think on those new things. Be God's fresh creation.
Jot down a good report. Read these scriptures
with a listening heart—ever mindful of
how much your Abba, Father, loves you.

In His Service

Therefore, as we have opportunity, let us do good to all people, especially to those who belong to the family of believers.

GALATIANS 6:10 NIV

In our hectic-paced life, it's often easy to overlook doing "good to all people." Our organized schedules don't always include opportunities to offer assistance to another. Maybe we should update our calendars and ink in ways to serve.

What opportunities exist for moms to show their children how to spread a bit of compassion? Look this day to see how you might reach out to those around you. If you're shy, start with people you already know. Take your children with you on an errand of mercy. Let them see the impact a caring heart has on another. Your shining example of service to others can be a beacon to those you love the most: your family.

From Page to Heart

. . . .

So Christ himself gave the apostles, the prophets,
the evangelists, the pastors and teachers,
to equip his people for works of service,
so that the body of Christ may be built up.
EPHESIANS 4:11–12 NIV

In Luke 10, there is a story about a Jewish traveler who is assaulted and left on the side of the road to die. A Samaritan came along— Samaritans were enemies of the Jews—and stopped to help the injured man. This man, labeled the Good Samaritan, saw a need and met it. No matter his plans, he assisted another.

God anointed Jesus of Nazareth with the Holy Spirit and power, and. . .he went around doing good and healing all who were under the power of the devil, because God was with him.
ACTS 10:38 NIV

The Bible teaches that God anointed Jesus with the Holy Spirit, and He went about doing good. When the Holy Spirit leads you, you will spot opportunities for service. Our lives should never be so busy that we cannot forgo some plans to help another.

For we are co-workers in God's service; you are God's field, God's building.
1 CORINTHIANS 3:9 NIV

Tuck these scriptures into your heart. Once you know the Holy Spirit resides there, He will guide and direct your way. Look around you. Do you see someone hurting or in need? Ask the Lord if that's the opportunity He opened up for you to serve Him. Be Jesus to another today.

Prayer

This, then, is how you should pray:
"'Our Father in heaven, hallowed be your
name, your kingdom come, your will be done,
on earth as it is in heaven. Give us today our
daily bread. And forgive us our debts,
as we also have forgiven our debtors.
And lead us not into temptation,
but deliver us from the evil one.'"
MATTHEW 6:9–13 NIV

If your child was away from home,
wouldn't you long to hear that youngster's
voice and know your child was doing well?
Then how much more does our heavenly
Father long to hear from us? It doesn't take
time on your knees to talk with Him. You may
communicate constantly.

Father God hears and knows your
heart. In answer to "how should we pray?"
Jesus gave His disciples the perfect answer,
recorded in Matthew 6. Let the words of this
scripture lift up your needs today.

From Page to Heart

. . . .

Devote yourselves to prayer,
being watchful and thankful.
COLOSSIANS 4:2 NIV

What could be more rewarding than teaching our children to pray? We know their tender hearts are malleable, and we might shape them "toward the Lord" so they learn to guard their hearts early on. Matthew 6:9–13, commonly referred to as the Lord's Prayer, is the pattern for the perfect prayer taught by Jesus. Learn those words with your children. Recite them together often, not in a rote fashion but in earnest prayer.

Do not be anxious about anything, but in every situation, by prayer and petition, with thanksgiving, present your requests to God. And the peace of God, which transcends all understanding, will guard your hearts and your minds in Christ Jesus.

<small>Philippians 4:6–7 niv</small>

Know your Abba, Father, cares about your deepest needs and desires. Burn these words from Philippians in your mind, for you will need to draw on their strength from time to time. We all tend to worry, but recognize God is in control of your days.

The prayer of a righteous person is powerful and effective.

<small>James 5:16 niv</small>

Find a prayer partner. Jesus said, "For where two or three gather in my name, there am I with them" (Matthew 18:20 NIV). Don't lose any opportunity to join with another and let your voices be heard. It doesn't take fancy words, for prayer is a conversation with the One who loves you the most.

"As the rain and the snow come down from heaven, and do not return to it without watering the earth and making it bud and flourish, so that it yields seed for the sower and bread for the eater, so is my word that goes out from my mouth: It will not return to me empty, but will accomplish what I desire and achieve the purpose for which I sent it."

ISAIAH 55:10–11 NIV

God's blessings are hard to miss when we open our eyes and notice. The air we breathe, the sun rising and setting, the glory of His handiwork. All nature should sing His praises. For He alone is worthy.

Remember what God has done for you. He alone knows what is in store for you and yours. He alone can be trusted. He alone holds His hand out to bless you.

Oh, Father, how we thank You!

From Page to Heart

. . . .

Praise be to the God and Father of our Lord Jesus Christ, who has blessed us in the heavenly realms with every spiritual blessing in Christ.

EPHESIANS 1:3 NIV

God, in His infinite wisdom, has chosen a path for you to walk. It's full of His goodness and blessing. But sometimes it takes spiritual eyes to recognize these blessings. We get mired down in our everyday comings and goings and find ourselves overwhelmed—and miss out on what He wants for us.

Blessed is the man who endures temptation;
for when he has been approved, he will receive
the crown of life which the Lord has
promised to those who love Him.
JAMES 1:12 NKJV

When we focus on circumstances surrounding us, we might not always feel blessed or see the Lord's hand of blessing. Often it takes discipline and courage to face what is ahead. Hide the words from scripture in your heart so you might call upon them when it's dark. Trust in His words. Lean on Him. For He has promised He will listen and be your guide.

Embrace your family and feel blessed this day

*"Bring the whole tithe into the storehouse,
that there may be food in my house. Test me
in this," says the Lord Almighty, "and see if
I will not throw open the floodgates of heaven
and pour out so much blessing that there
will not be room enough to store it."*

MALACHI 3:10 NIV

Secure in Him

He will be the sure foundation for your times,
a rich store of salvation and wisdom
and knowledge; the fear of the LORD
is the key to this treasure.
ISAIAH 33:6 NIV

As moms, we want our children to feel secure, safe, and confident as they walk through life. Yet when we open the front door and send them out, the world wants to swallow them. Therefore, we must put their feet upon the Firm Foundation—Jesus—so, when the winds of adversity blow or trouble threatens, they know where to go.

Having the Word deep within will give you and yours a well upon which you may draw. Be assured the Holy Spirit guards that which you love with a fierce protectiveness. Rest in His love.

O dear Father, we want to feel Your arms about us. Let us lean on You, sheltered and safe. Amen.

From Page to Heart

. . . .

The LORD is good, a refuge in times of trouble.
He cares for those who trust in him.

NAHUM 1:7 NIV

LORD, you alone are my portion and my cup;
you make my lot secure.

PSALM 16:5 NIV

If you watch the evening news, you might be tempted to pull the covers over your head and stay in bed. There is so much unrest in the world. How do we, as Christians, deal with all the problems that we face? With prayer and coming to know His heart and His desires for our lives.

*The Lord is my rock, my fortress and my
deliverer; my God is my rock, in whom
I take refuge, my shield and the horn
of my salvation, my stronghold.*

PSALM 18:2 NIV

Scripture speaks of God hiding Moses in the cleft of the rock (see Exodus 33:22), and even of believers resting on His shoulders. What amazing word pictures. Speak them forth. If your voice trembles, He still hears. Know God will shelter you with love.

*"Let the beloved of the Lord rest secure in him,
for he shields him all day long, and the one
the Lord loves rests between his shoulders."*

DEUTERONOMY 33:12 NIV

Does this mean bad things won't happen?

No, most certainly not. It just means we know how to handle times of strife and stress. We know to reach up and grab the Father's hand and follow the path He puts before us.

"Do not be anxious about your life, what you will eat or what you will drink, nor about your body, what you will put on. Is not life more than food, and the body more than clothing?
Look at the birds of the air: they neither sow nor reap nor gather into barns, and yet your heavenly Father feeds them. . . .
And which of you by being anxious can add a single hour to his span of life? . . .
Consider the lilies of the field."

MATTHEW 6:25–28 ESV

The British evangelist Alan Redpath stated, "I refuse to become panicky, as I lift up my eyes to Him and accept it as coming from the throne of God for some great purpose of blessing to my own heart." Oh, Father, if we could always become so grounded in Your goodness that when adversity strikes, our first thought is of You.

From Page to Heart

· ·

Consider it pure joy, my brothers and sisters,
whenever you face trials of many kinds,
because you know that the testing
of your faith produces perseverance.
JAMES 1:2–3 NIV

*W*arning: danger ahead. Wouldn't it be amazing to always have a sign that gave us a heads up on trouble? We might arm ourselves, steady our hands, and be ready to handle anything—in our own power. So how is that working? For most of us, not so well. It's hard to juggle a family and meet all their daily demands. We try to call upon our Wonder Woman powers and can't always find them. Panic ensues. That overwhelming feeling wells up and worry sets in. But look ahead to this scripture:

For I am the L<small>ORD</small> your God who takes
hold of your right hand and says to you,
Do not fear; I will help you.
I<small>SAIAH</small> 41:13 <small>NIV</small>

Calm down. Make a list. Take a deep breath.
For the Holy Spirit is beside you to guide your
path. Scripture promises us help! He's got our
right hand in His, and with the right focus, there's
nothing we can't accomplish.

"The Lord is my helper; I will not be afraid.
What can mere mortals do to me?"
H<small>EBREWS</small> 13:6 <small>NIV</small>

Rest in Him. As the old hymn says,
"Turn your eyes upon Jesus, look full in His
wonderful face, and the things of earth will grow
strangely dim, in the light of His glory and grace."

*Love is patient, love is kind. It does not
envy, it does not boast, it is not proud.
It does not dishonor others, it is not
self-seeking, it is not easily angered,
it keeps no record of wrongs. Love does not
delight in evil but rejoices with the truth.
It always protects, always trusts, always hopes,
always perseveres. Love never fails. But where
there are prophecies, they will cease; where
there are tongues, they will be stilled;
where there is knowledge, it will pass away.*

1 CORINTHIANS 13:4–8 NIV

Billy Graham once said, "God is more
interested in your future and your
relationships than you are." God has a great
investment in our lives, and we need to
recognize His care and love.

People will let us down. That is a given.
God never will. Make sure your relationship
with the Creator is on solid ground.

From Page to Heart

· · · · · · · · · · · · · · · · · · · ·

Children, obey your parents in the Lord,
for this is right. "Honor your father and mother"—
which is the first commandment with a promise—
"so that it may go well with you and that
you may enjoy long life on the earth."

EPHESIANS 6:1–3 NIV

Mother-child relationships can be complicated. Tiny babies become messy toddlers, whining double-digits, rebellious teens. Mom, as the "heart of the home," struggles to bring order and discipline into this rocky household.

Start children off on the way they should go,
and even when they are old they
will not turn from it.
PROVERBS 22:6 NIV

Training your child in the Word can enable your youngster to walk a more godly path, to make better life choices, to have assurance the Holy Spirit is within. Learn scriptures with your child. Repeat them, pray them, so when your child needs to hear from the Spirit, His voice will come through loud and clear.

Compassion

When he saw the crowds, he had compassion on them, because they were harassed and helpless, like sheep without a shepherd.
MATTHEW 9:36 NIV

Does your heart hurt and do your eyes well up with tears for another? Are you able to sense deep down inside how a friend or relative feels? That is experiencing compassion, an empathy that enables you to better pray for that person.

There are appropriate times to let your children join you in prayers for the suffering of another. It teaches them kindness and care for others. What a legacy to have children who care for others through prayer in this world that can be so coldhearted.

Talk with your children this day and gently explain your sense of sympathy. Then pray with them in a manner in which they will understand.

From Page to Heart

. . . .

Be kind to one another, tenderhearted, forgiving
one another, even as God in Christ forgave you.
EPHESIANS 4:32 NKJV

Compassion is a key part of spirituality. The
definition of *compassion* is: "a feeling of deep
sympathy or sorrow for another who is stricken
with misfortune, accompanied by the strong desire
to alleviate the suffering."

But you, Lord, are a compassionate
and gracious God, slow to anger,
abounding in love and faithfulness.
PSALM 86:15 NIV

From Genesis until the final conclusion of Revelation, we see a God who designed a world just for us, only to have us sin against Him. Yet, He doesn't stop there. Instead He pursues us and brings all who believe in Jesus in to a right relationship with God through the blood shed by His Son. That is compassion, when someone who knew no sin became sin for us and died on a cross so that we could have life eternal with God!

Bear ye one another's burdens,
and so fulfil the law of Christ.
GALATIANS 6:2 KJV

While we probably won't die for another, walking alongside someone in a time of need is an amazing experience. Albert Schweitzer once stated, "The purpose of human life is to serve, and to show compassion and the will to help others." Our hearts become tender and our lives are more fulfilled when we reach out to the hurting. Let your child learn this lesson—to care for others.

Are You Listening?

*"Behold, I stand at the door and knock.
If anyone hears my voice and opens
the door, I will come in to him and eat
with him, and he with me."*
REVELATION 3:20 ESV

*O*nce you have opened the door of your
heart and let the Lord Jesus in, your walk
with Him begins. You have a Companion
and Guide who will walk alongside you
forever. Just as you can have a tour guide on
vacation, you listen and learn. So, too, will the
Holy Spirit lead you in God's way.

Tune your ears to hear what Jesus says.
Become familiar with the Word and hide it deep
in your heart. Pass it on to your children so they
may see and hear the wonders of God.

Christ's voice sounds for us in loving
invitation; and dead in sin. . .though we be,
we can listen and live.
ALEXANDER MCLAREN

From Page to Heart

. . . .

So faith comes from hearing,
and hearing through the word of Christ.
ROMANS 10:17 ESV

⁓

*R*emember the first cries of your newborn—how they awakened you from a deep sleep? Your listening heart was attuned to that little one, ready to jump up and serve in any way that child needed. Once we begin our walk of faith, we can know our Abba, Father, hears us just as we heard our children. His ear is tuned to us, so ours must be to Him.

And this is the confidence that we have
toward him, that if we ask anything
according to his will he hears us.
1 JOHN 5:14 ESV

Scripture promises you may see wondrous things when you attune yourself to His way. You may ask and hear from Him. But listening does not occur naturally; it is a result of a conscious choice. Although it may appear to be ordinary and easy, it is not. Jesus visited the home of Mary and Martha and chided Martha for her busyness; while Mary sat at His feet and listened, Martha bustled about.

Trust in the Lord with all your heart and lean not on your own understanding; in all your ways submit to him, and he will make your paths straight.
PROVERBS 3:5–6 NIV

Don't be too busy to listen for His voice.
The soft whisper of the Holy Spirit will lead you
to the path of righteousness. Hear Him today!

The LORD is gracious and compassionate,
slow to anger and rich in love.
PSALM 145:8 NIV

∽

Refrain from anger, and forsake wrath!
Fret not yourself; it tends only to evil.
PSALMS 37:8 ESV

*M*ahatma Ghandi stated, "It is easier to build a boy than to mend a man." Of all the things in the human heart, anger can be one of the most intense, destructive, and unhealthy emotions we can experience. Anger may be caused by pressures of work, family, or even from being the innocent victim of another's wrongdoing. Left unresolved, anger creates an intense desire to destroy something. If not handled in the proper way, it can have drastic, life-changing consequences.

It's time to examine your life and find the root of anger. Not in-the-moment anger, but deep, unresolved issues. Take these to the Lord in prayer, and let the Holy Spirit minister to your heart.

From Page to Heart

Whoever is patient has great understanding.
PROVERBS 14:29 NIV

Most moms experience anger in an average week. Whether it's caused by a spilled glass of milk, an unkind word, or an overdue bill, anger can well up until a valve is required to release the pressure. Don't let that valve open onto your children. An angry word can scar a child for life! Take a deep breath and find a quiet spot—maybe your closet or car—before you explode. The count-to-ten rule never hurts.

My dear brothers and sisters, take note of this: Everyone should be quick to listen, slow to speak and slow to become angry, because human anger does not produce the righteousness that God desires.
JAMES 1:19–20 NIV

Toddlers or older children are going to mess up. It doesn't mean you have to react in a fury. Inappropriate actions never pay off. And it takes great discipline to follow the words in James. It's not easy to control the tongue.

Be angry and do not sin; do not let the sun go down on your anger, and give no opportunity to the devil.
 EPHESIANS 4:26–27 ESV

Examine the day at nightfall. Maybe you need to say I'm sorry. Then take the events to the Lord in prayer. Let the Holy Spirit soothe your ruffled feelings and comfort you. It might be time to journal your thoughts and emotions so you can see your growth as you lean on Him.

Obey

*"The LORD our God, the LORD is one. You shall
love the LORD your God with all your heart and
with all your soul and with all your might.
And these words that I command you today
shall be on your heart. You shall teach them
diligently to your children, and shall talk of them
when you sit in your house, and when you walk
by the way, and when you lie down,
and when you rise."*

DEUTERONOMY 6:4–7 ESV

The word *obey* in Greek means "to listen
attentively," by implication "to heed or con-
form to a command or authority." The idea is to
actively follow a command, no choice involved.

God gave us His guidebook and expects
us to read and understand His instructions.
Just as we expect our children to listen
without question—stay out of the street,
don't run with scissors—our Lord God
expects the same.

From Page to Heart

For He will give His angels [especial] charge over you to accompany and defend and preserve you in all your ways [of obedience and service].
PSALM 91:11 AMP

*H*ave you laid out rules for your children to follow? Aren't those rules ones that are for their good, not harm—ones that you've lovingly designed? And don't you expect your children to obey? In the same manner, our Abba, Father, expects us to obey His words.

If you [really] love Me, you will keep (obey) My commands.
JOHN 14:15 AMP

That's what scripture lays out for us, special rules that will help us in our walk with the Lord. They aren't there to trip us up or keep us from a good life. Instead, the gracious Lord, in His great mercy, has outlined our own unique path.

Blessed is the man who walks not in the counsel of the wicked, nor stands in the way of sinners, nor sits in the seat of scoffers; but his delight is in the law of the Lord, and on his law he meditates day and night.
PSALM 1:1–2 ESV

When we do as this psalm suggests and mediate on this law, we will come to recognize those areas where we might stumble. We will appreciate the "lamp unto [our] feet" the Creator left for us (Psalm 119:105 KJV). Begin letting the Word sink in and saturate you today. Obedience is a key ingredient to a contented life.

Frustration

"For I know the plans I have for you, declares the Lord, plans for welfare and not for evil, to give you a future and a hope. Then you will call upon me and come and pray to me, and I will hear you. You will seek me and find me, when you seek me with all your heart."
Jeremiah 29:11–13 ESV

Synonyms for *frustration* include: *aggravation, irritation, disturbance,* and *dissatisfaction*. Do those words describe you today?

Our lives get so cluttered that we often forget to look heavenward, to seek advice from the King of kings. Then we try to "work it out on our own." That tactic often leads to failure then frustration.

See in the Word that God has a plan for you. Rest in assurance, knowing full well that His way is best. Nothing happens in your life that surprises the Lord. He's orchestrated your days. Praise His name.

From Page to Heart

. . . .

Do not be dismayed, for I am your God.
I will strengthen you and help you;
I will uphold you with my righteous right hand.
ISAIAH 41:10 NIV

Feeling frustrated is most often a sign of discontentment. Life is not necessarily going our way. Like two-year-olds, we'd like to stomp our feet, shake our fists, and cry, "Do it *my* way! Right now!" It's difficult to rein in those emotions and collect ourselves. But it's necessary.

Cast all your anxiety on him because
he cares for you.
1 PETER 5:7 NIV

Don't worry about what's next. Rest in His love and wait to see what He will unfold for you. Trusting is the key.

Now faith is the assurance of things hoped for, the conviction of things not seen.
HEBREWS 11:1 ESV

Talk with your children about these verses.
Speak the words over them. God is love.

Patience

Moreover [let us also be full of joy now!]
let us exult and triumph in our troubles
and rejoice in our sufferings, knowing that
pressure and affliction and hardship produce
patient and unswerving endurance.
ROMANS 5:3 AMP

*A*rnold H. Glasow wrote: "The key to everything is patience. You get the chicken by hatching the egg, not by smashing it." Our staying power will surely be tested as moms. Full of joy? It's hard to live without complaining about things that go wrong. Let's learn to lift our voices in praise and try to understand what it means to wait upon the Lord.

Sometimes we think we want to know when God's going to move in our lives. We'd like to see the whole plan so we know what's coming. It's not easy when things get stagnant. That is the very time to saturate our hearts with the Word.

From Page to Heart

. . . .

*But the fruit of the Spirit is love, joy, peace,
patience, kindness, goodness, faithfulness.*
GALATIANS 5:22 ESV

Scripture outlines such a beautiful picture of
patience in Galatians. Yet we often fall short of
that list of fruit. Instead, we find ourselves tapping
one foot and grumbling about life's restraints.
Today, when you tap that foot, use the beat of the
words and repeat *His* Word.

*Be joyful in hope, patient in affliction,
faithful in prayer.*

Romans 12:12 niv

*But they who wait for the Lord shall renew
their strength; they shall mount up with wings
like eagles; they shall run and not be weary;
they shall walk and not faint.*

Isaiah 40:31 esv

Waiting is never easy. The Lord knows we need His strength, goodness, and mercy to make it through a day. Let's rest in Him and feel the presence of the Holy Spirit.

Rushing, Hurried, Harried

*In the morning, L*ORD*, you hear my voice;*
in the morning I lay my requests before
you and wait expectantly.

PSALM 5:3 NIV

King David knew his need of daily time
alone with God, and, though faced
with trials and pressures that were pulling
him in other directions, he vowed that
nothing would keep him from meeting with
God—especially at the beginning of his
day. In Psalm 5:3 (NLT) David vowed: "Each
morning I bring my requests to you and wait
expectantly."

No doubt it was this intimate morning-
by-morning meeting with the Lord that
developed David's faith and made him a
man after God's own heart (see 1 Samuel
13:14). Unless we make time alone with God a
priority, the other hours devoted to our busy
schedules will be poorly used.

From Page to Heart

. . . .

*"Come to me, all who labor and are heavy laden,
and I will give you rest. Take my yoke upon you,
and learn from me, for I am gentle and lowly in
heart, and you will find rest for your souls.
For my yoke is easy, and my burden is light."*
MATTHEW 11:28–29 ESV

Finding time to get alone with God is a need for
all Christians—wives and mothers, husbands
and fathers, children, students—everyone. Why?
Because it is through seclusion with God that we
are able to develop and maintain the mind of the
Spirit and keep our spiritual equilibrium so that
God is at the center and in control of our lives.
Write the scriptures in your journal or on note
cards so they might sink into your heart.

I will meditate on Your precepts,
and contemplate Your ways.
PSALM 119:15 NKJV

❧

For people will reap what they sow (see Galatians 6:7). Just as a farmer is helpless to grow his crop without preparing the soil and sowing the seed, so we must prepare the soil of our hearts and sow the seed of the Word in order to reap a harvest of righteousness.

We need to learn scripture and its truth, and, for maximum impact, we need to get into the Word daily. In this way, Bible study becomes a first-hand, personal experience rather than simply second-hand knowledge from someone else.

Joy

*Then Peter said, "Silver or gold I do not have,
but what I do have I give you. . . ." [The man]
jumped to his feet and began to walk.
Then he went with them into the temple
courts, walking and jumping,
and praising God.*
ACTS 3:6, 8 NIV

~~~

*H*ave you ever experienced something so
magnificent that your heart felt full and
you wanted to shout for joy? Imagine this
man who was healed. He'd been lame from
birth and now could walk!

Joy sometimes cannot be contained. Let
it spill forth and revel in it. Draw from the well
of contentment and sing His praises. Teach
your children the "thank You, Lord" attitude!

Just as David sang while in exile, learn to
look for the joyful moments. Point them out
to your family. Record them for days when
you feel blue. "For the joy of the Lord is your
strength" (Nehemiah 8:10 NIV).

From Page to Heart

. . . .

The LORD is my strength and my shield;
my heart trusts in him, and he helps me. My heart
leaps for joy, and with my song I praise him.
PSALM 28:7 NIV

*W*hat more needs to be said? When our hearts do trust in our Creator, we can gladly sing to Him for all the great things He has done. We can say, "Let our words be sweet, sweet sounds in Your ears!"

Shout for joy to the Lᴏʀᴅ, all the earth.
Worship the Lᴏʀᴅ with gladness; come before him
with joyful songs. Know that the Lᴏʀᴅ is God.
It is he who made us, and we are his; we are his
people, the sheep of his pasture. Enter his gates
with thanksgiving and his courts with praise;
give thanks to him and praise his name. For the
Lᴏʀᴅ is good and his love endures forever; his
faithfulness continues through all generations.
Psᴀʟᴍ 100:1–5 ɴɪᴠ

Recite Psalm 100 as you march around your
house, children in tow: a great army for the Lord.
We find pleasure when our children run to us with
an unexpected hug or kiss, and so it is with the
Lord. He delights in us!

Find time in your day to smile at Him, to recognize His gifts and give Him the praise He deserves. Teach your children to say thank You to Him during their day. This will enrich their lives as they learn gratitude can sprinkle much joy in their lives.

Peace

*When you pass through the waters, I will be
with you; and when you pass through the
rivers, they will not sweep over you.
When you walk through the fire, you will not
be burned; the flames will not set you ablaze.*

ISAIAH 43:2 NIV

~

*A*ccepting Jesus Christ as your Savior gives
you the right to call yourself a child of the
King. As your right, your inheritance, you will
receive protection and love from the Father.
You are safe. Nothing will snatch you from
His hands.

Let your heart rest in Him with the
knowledge He is working all things together
for your good (see Romans 8:28). Take a
deep breath and feel the peace wash over
you. Relinquish control. Surrender.

Be calm. The Holy Spirit will whisper His
love and His directions for your path. Trust.
Obey. And live in peace, despite the storms
that might surround you; He holds your hand.

From Page to Heart

. . . .

*For God gave us a spirit not of fear but of power
and love and self-control.*
2 Timothy 1:7 ESV

Fear can overwhelm you at unexpected
moments. Drawing upon scripture will help you
tamp down any emotions that lead to fear. Learn
the words of our Lord and Savior. Recall them when
fear rises. Call upon Him and know He hears you.
Repeat these words until they seep into your heart.

David was in fear for his life for years. He
learned early on who his Redeemer and Friend
was, who would give him peace in any situation.
Too often our fears overwhelm us at night, as we
try to sleep. Call upon David's words when your
head hits the pillow:

*Many, L*ORD*, are asking, "Who will bring us prosperity?" Let the light of your face shine on us. Fill my heart with joy. . . . In peace I will lie down and sleep, for you alone, L*ORD*, make me dwell in safety.*

PSALM 4:6–8 NIV

Like a nightlight, God's Word spills forth.

"The LORD make his face shine on you and be gracious to you; the LORD turn his face toward you and give you peace."
NUMBERS 6:25–26 NIV

*For the LORD will be at your side and will keep
your foot from being snared.*
PROVERBS 3:26 NIV

Faith means "confidence, trust, reliance,
assurance"—wonderful words that can
fill our hearts. To step out in faith or rely on
our faith can be a scary deal. This is when
our belief in the Lord is most tested. In the
privacy of our homes, we show our faith to
our children. But in the big outside world, it's
often put under a microscope.

Your faithfulness, your loyalty to God, will
be tested. That is why pouring scripture into
your heart is so important. It backs up your
emotions with facts, so if you are challenged,
you will have the answer.

A. W. Tozer stated: "True faith rests upon
the character of God and asks no further
proof. . . . It is enough that God said it."

From Page to Heart

*For it is by grace you have been saved,
through faith—and this is not from yourselves,
it is the gift of God.*

EPHESIANS 2:8 NIV

The most effective weapon we have to overcome
difficult situations is a strong bond of faith in
God. When we are saved, we can call upon our
heavenly Father at any time, for anything. He
knows our needs and hears our cries. The Lord
Jesus bends low to hear our prayers. When we
hide these words in our hearts, we know for sure
He rides on the clouds, coming swiftly, as it says in
Isaiah 19:1.

He [Jesus] replied. . . "Truly I tell you, if you have faith as small as a mustard seed, you can say to this mountain, 'Move from here to there,' and it will move. Nothing will be impossible for you."
MATTHEW 17:20 NIV

Write down these wonderful words of life! Engrave them on your heart. Nothing is impossible for Him! Hard to imagine, isn't it? Teach this concept to your children so they know Abba, Father, hears them. Pray with them, rejoicing when answered prayer happens. Nothing is more important than sowing the words of scripture into their lives.

Therefore, since we have been justified through faith, we have peace with God through our Lord Jesus Christ.
ROMANS 5:1 NIV

Dear Lord, how we thank You for the sacrifice
of Your Son on our behalf. We put our faith
and trust in You. Amen.

Tell Others

"Go therefore and make disciples of all nations, baptizing them in the name of the Father and of the Son and of the Holy Spirit, teaching them to observe all that I have commanded you. And behold, I am with you always, to the end of the age."

MATTHEW 28:19–20 ESV

When you were pregnant with your first child, were you filled with excitement? Did you want to grab your phone, call and text the news to your friends and family? One girl took a picture of herself holding a sign that read "I'm pregnant" and wrapped it in a gift box. Imagine Nana's surprise when she opened the package.

The word *gospel* means "good news"! During the time of Jesus, couriers went from town to town with reports of battles won, nations conquered. And they spread the news.

It's time to spread the news of what Jesus has done for you!

From Page to Heart

. . . .

He said to them, "Do you bring in a lamp
to put it under a bowl or a bed? Instead,
don't you put it on its stand?"
MARK 4:21 NIV

*B*efore Jesus ascended to heaven, He
commanded His disciples to tell others about
Him. And now we must spread the word. You may
ask, "Why me? Aren't there others better equipped
to do that? I'm not a preacher, I don't know what
to say."

But you will receive power when
the Holy Spirit comes on you.
ACTS 1:8 NIV

Christ commanded us to tell others about Him and promised to give us power to do it through the Holy Spirit. Just like witnesses in a legal proceeding, we are asked to be His witnesses on earth. We are to testify to the things we've personally seen and heard.

Think what it is that we have received. To know Jesus Christ as Savior and Lord is the greatest thing in all of life's experiences. You are the only one who knows what happened. No one can adequately describe the wonderful things that have changed in your life since you have surrendered yourself to Christ. First share with your children, your family, then ripple out from your household. Rejoice!

It is your story; no one else can tell it.

Scripture Index